Lingerie

Page 4:
"Volupté" ensemble
under wire bra and panties.
Chantelle creation. Fall/ Winter 2003

Page 6:
Chantal Thomass
Collection Fall/ Winter 2001-2002

Designed by :
Baseline Co Ltd
19-25 Nguyen Hue
Bitexco Building, Floor 11
District 1, Ho Chi Minh City
Vietnam

ISBN 1-84013-729-0

Published in 2005 by Grange Books
an imprint of Grange Books Plc
The Grange Kingsnorth Industrial Estate
Hoo, nr Rochester, Kent ME3 9ND
www.grangebooks.co.uk

Foreword

"Know, first, who you are, and then adorn yourself accordingly."

— Epictetus

L ingerie is directly and very strongly related to a woman's intimacy. For centuries, men have always believed that lingerie was created with the aim of seducing them. This desire to seduce undeniably exists.

However, in choosing to wear pretty and seductive underwear, women behave and carry themselves in a slightly egoistic and indeed narcissistic way. Furthermore, lingerie can help a woman feel good about her body, helping her thus to like and accept it, and in doing this, affirming a real sense of self-confidence. The reason behind it is simple. Surprisingly, although no-one can see our underwear, it contributes effectively in enhancing our silhouette and sometimes even shaping it to our personal preferences.

All too often, lingerie has been treated as an object of seduction. Men themselves have created this phenomenon: to see a woman uniquely dressed in underwear is infinitely more sensual and sexual than seeing a woman entirely naked. One could associate lingerie with high heels for the latter effect, the way in which a woman walks, making her more seductive, charming and provocative.

Associated with stockings, high heels have a power, an obvious fetishist virtue, for both men and women. The perception and judgement of the female body has gone through changes over the years, if one compares for example, our time, the beginning of the 21st century, to the years between 1960 and 1970.

In the 1960s, when a woman married, and moreover when she became a mother, her body could no longer be considered seductive. Today, this outlook is completely old-fashioned and obsolete. Women feel the need to be attractive, whatever their age, whether it be prior to marriage or after, and even in the years later.

As proof, a grandmother today can still be a beautiful woman and feel it by dressing herself in some appealing underwear, which enables her to make her body more beautiful. This evolution (or revolution?) of morals concerning lingerie is directly related to the innovations and technical contingencies in the creation of underwear, and the subjection to historical events. The history of lingerie deserves to be put in the spotlight. Lingerie, in contrast with the world of fashion, is a state of mind. One can love lingerie and envy looking after one's body whether one is 15 or 75! The world of prêt-à-porter is a completely different universe from that of the world of underwear.

Clothes always target a particular age group: the fashion of a teenage 15 year-old is different from that of a 30 year-old woman.

This is why lingerie is more a question of mentality and of human nature. A plump woman can feel good in her body, accept who she is and have a desire to emphasize that beauty by wearing gorgeous underwear. Lingerie should respond to all these aspirations and suit every kind of woman. A designer's work should be orientated towards this fulfilment.

Pair of stays

first half of the 17th century
Iron, Inv. 2002.2.X
Leloir Fund, Musée Galliera, Paris

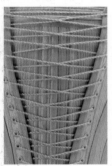

To create lingerie that satisfies different women's' styles, one should observe those women who surround you: daughters, assistants, even women in the street! Poses, which one notices in films, can also help to inspire. Besides those who surround, who play an important role in suggesting new designs, the material is also a source of inspiration.

Pair of stays

English, c. 1660-70
pink watered silk backed with linen stiffened
with whalebone and trimmed with pink silk ribbons
Victoria and Albert Museum, London

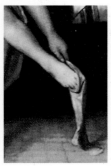

The fabrics are essential. Lingerie is the type of clothing worn closest to the female body and is in contact with its intimacy, the fabrics and lace have to be agreeable, but not exclusively. Today, lingerie has to be comfortable and practical. If it was 30 years ago, French women (in contrast with American women, for example) accepted and did not balk at wearing and hand-washing a piece of delicate lingerie, with lace, which even needed ironing at times. Today, that is no longer acceptable.

The Morning Toilet

Jan Steen, c.1663
Oil on wood, 64.7 x 53 cm
Royal collection, London

13

Lingerie should be machine-washable, with no need for ironing, and should incorporate all the essential elements of comfort, with the beauty of the creations. The evolution of different textiles used in the creation and the making of underwear remains an unforgettable aspect. Besides the materials, the colour of lingerie plays an important role too.

The Toilet

François Boucher, 1742
Oil on canvas, 52.5 x 65.5 cm
Thyssen-Bornemisza collection, Madrid

Black and white are always extremely flattering colours for the skin. Black, (more particularly) allows the softening of bodily flaws that we all have. Hot colours (pink, red, raspberry) are also enhancing colours. On the other hand, cold colours used for lingerie are always more difficult to work with. Greens and blues are magnificent, but all too often evoke swimming costumes.

Body with whalebone
_____

18th century
Fabric decorated with flowers, Inv. 1920.1.1856
Leloir Fund, Musée Galliera, Paris

Lingerie should be associated with women's' pleasure. The element of seduction remains, especially with certain pieces of underwear, which are not trivial. Certain pieces are fascinating and provoke an inevitable attraction. Stockings and suspenders make a woman extremely enticing, indeed entrancing. Strapless bras, girdles and bras can be worn under a transparent blouse.

"Undressed for the bath"

Anonymous, 18th century
Engraving from the series "Baths and Toilets"
Musée Carnavalet, Paris

19

This could produce a mysterious and clashing effect and can be fascinating to the eyes of others and overtly flattering for the woman who dress in this way. There are two kinds of lingerie in my opinion. On the one hand, a woman has the underwear that she desires to show (girdles, suspenders and stockings), and on the other hand the kind of underwear that one wears uniquely for oneself.

Baths and Toilets #7
———————————————

Anonymous, 18th century
Engraving
Musée Carnavalet, Paris

21

This latter category should be pleasant for the eye, but also extremely comfortable. Concerning tights, for example, I believe it is very important to make tights which are charming and delicious, so that one could wear them every day and be able, despite everything else, to conserve a seductive power, when one undresses in the presence of a man.

Baths and Toilets no.10

Anonymous, 18th century
Engraving
Musée Carnavalet, Paris

23

Lingerie is all about being oneself and about one's attitude. Three terms can be associated with lingerie today: refinement, seduction and comfort. It is necessary to put together these three notions in order to create underwear, excluding vulgarity along the way. To avoid this pitfall, one has to contribute humour and purity.

Woman's underwear

English, c.1770-1780 and 1778 respectively
Fine linen shift corset or red silk,
damask and side hoop pink striped linen
Victoria and Albert Museum, London

The world of lingerie affects everyone. It affects women who wear lingerie, as well as the men who have always believed that they wear it to seduce them. Lingerie deserves to have a greater place in history, as well as in everyday life. Intimate apparel comes in many guises. It can be hidden or exposed, simple or sophisticated, discrete or provocative.

Factory of crinolines: the making of hoops

Bach
Engraving
Musée Carnavalet, Paris

The vast array is traditionally divided into three groups: lingerie, corsetry, and hosiery. Underwear serves a mainly hygienic function. Positioned between the body and its clothing, underwear shields the body from garments made of less comfortable textiles and protects the clothing from body fluids, which is why each epoch produces underwear in various healthful fabrics.

"Le coucher des ouvrières en linge"
(The bedtime of the lingerie workers)

c.1801
Engraving, 15 x 19.2 cm
Maciet collection
Bibliothèque des Arts décoratifs, Paris

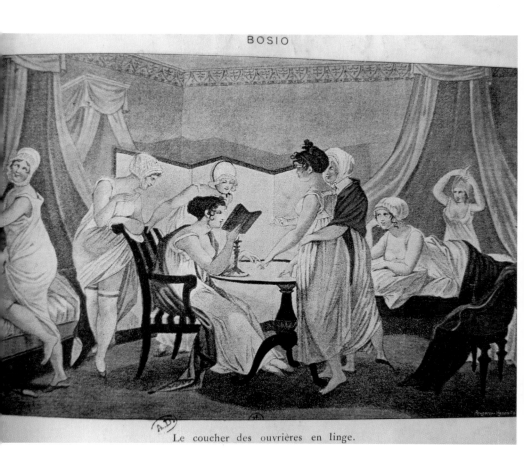

Le coucher des ouvrières en linge.

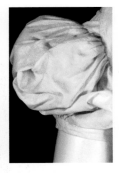

Women's underwear is therefore closely associated with intimacy and feminine hygiene: the first articles of lingerie in contact with the female body were worn in the context of menstruation and evolved into the contemporary sanitary napkin. The word underwear is synonymous with lingerie, the term used to refer to specific undergarments such as petticoats and camisoles, and later bloomers, leggings, underpants, undershirts, and full-length slips.

Corset

———

c.1820
White cotton, Inv. 1957.16.17
Leloir Fund, Musée Galliera, Paris

In families of modest means and during wartime, some articles of lingerie were made from worn-out household linens (usually old bed sheets), because underwear and household linens were made from similar materials. Among these fabrics comfort is the common denominator with cotton the most popular choice for its softness, lightness, and hygienic qualities.

"Le Bon Genre N°30"
Grisettes' Bedtime

c.1830
Private collection, Paris

E. 53/4.(44.)A.03.   DERNAVAL.SC

Le Bon Genre, N.° 30.

33

Other more or less delicate fabrics came to be used for making lingerie: linen, silk, and synthetic fabrics in relatively light weaves such as plain and satin weave, jersey, lawn, muslin, percale, and voile. These fabrics are sometimes found trimmed with decorative and frequently seductive details. For lingerie is not limited to a protective function – it is also a sophisticated costume accessory.

"Eight o'clock in the evening"

Achille Deveria, c.1830
Les Heures de la Parisienne
Musée Galliera, Paris

Underclothes assume the status of over-clothes when lingerie is partially revealed or fully exposed through flirtatiousness, fashion, or provocation, in which case it flaunts the characteristic frills and flounces of coquetry in the form of lace, embroidery, and ribbons. Lingerie colours vary according to the woman wearing it, changing as a function of her age, status, social role, taste, intended effect, and as fashion dictates.

Ladies underwear

English 1835 and 1834 respectively
Linen shift and cotton drawers
Victoria and Albert Museum, London

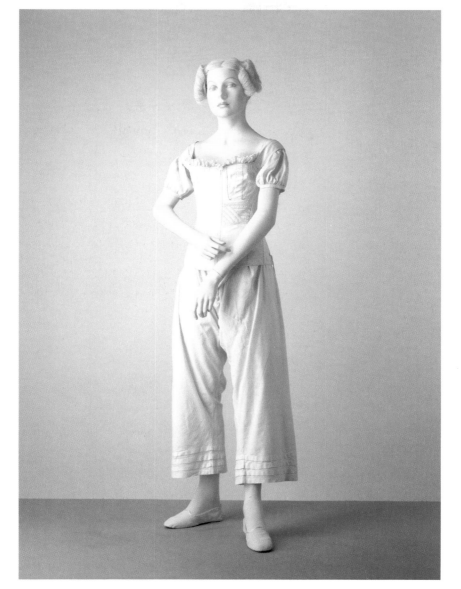

But lingerie is only rarely fully displayed due to its association with nudity, as demonstrated by Georges Feydeau's play, *Put Some Clothes On, Clarisse!* in which Ventroux chastises his wife for appearing in front of her son in a camisole. "That is completely see-through!" he tells her. Clarisse replies that she cannot be nude because she is wearing her camisole.

"Trop peu ! Trop !"
(Too much! Too little!)

_____

Charles Vernier, 1855
Engraving, *Charivari*
Musée Galliera, Paris

Trop peu !   Trop !

The episode demonstrates that from a woman's perspective lingerie provides coverage, whereas the male sees the nudity underneath. Because of its contact with skin and its close association with feminine intimacy, lingerie was and remains an object of fantasy among men, discretely fostered by the women who wear it.

"Utilité de la crinoline"
(Of the utility of crinoline)

Charles Vernier, 1855
Engraving, *Charivari*
Musée Galliera, Paris

Imp^{on} Martinet 172, r Rivoli et 41, r Vivienne   Lith Destouches, 28, r Paradis P^{le} Paris.

UTILITE DE LA CRINOLINE

_ C'est ça, garantis tes filles …. moi , je me charge de ton chapeau et de ta robe …., ça m'a coûté assez cher !…

Glimpsing petticoat flounces in the 18th and 19th centuries had the same impact on the male observer's imagination as making out the panties or string under a young woman's jeans today. Lingerie is erotically charged precisely because it is the most private aspect of femininity. The corsetry category belongs more to the realm of disguise.

Underwear of cotton chemise, whalebone corset of blue silk and crinoline spring. Steel hoop frame covered with braid with horsehair frill

English and French, c.1860-1869
Victoria and Albert Museum, London

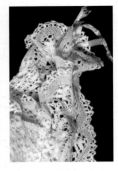

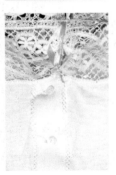

The relationship of corsetry to clothing is like that of a structural frame to a building, except in the case of corsetry the framework is positioned over a pre-existing foundation: the female body. The role of corsetry is to mold the figure and to impose the shapes of fashion upon it. To this end corsetry is used to transform three key body parts: waist, bust, and hips, the three areas upon which a new silhouette is constructed.

Corset concealer

Stiches and lace
Musées d'Art et d'Histoire, Troyes

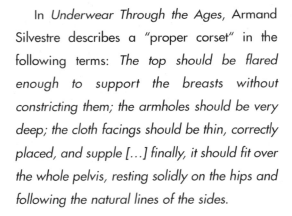

In *Underwear Through the Ages*, Armand Silvestre describes a "proper corset" in the following terms: *The top should be flared enough to support the breasts without constricting them; the armholes should be very deep; the cloth facings should be thin, correctly placed, and supple [...] finally, it should fit over the whole pelvis, resting solidly on the hips and following the natural lines of the sides.*

Crinoline underskirt

---

c.1865
White cotton, wicker frame, Inv.2003.75.X
Musée Galliera, Paris

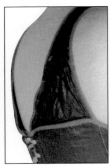

Corsetry thus accentuates the body's natural curves and enables the figure to conform to new lines. It can give a round, uplifted, shapely, or flat bust; a more or less slender, invisible, or extremely obvious waist; and it can slim down or widen the hips. Imposing the demands of fashion upon the body, corsetry often goes against nature.

Sport or summer corset
and underskirt with bustle (called "crabtail")

1875-80
Inv. 1920.1.968 Inv. 2003.73.X
Musée Galliera, Paris

And as much as lingerie belongs to the realm of intimacy, corsetry is tied to external appearance. It is her corsetry that turns a woman wearing a dress into a fashion plate. The corsetry category includes underclothes such as whalebone bodies, corsets, girdles, guêpières, bustiers, farthingales, panniers, and crinolines. A piece of corsetry is made up of internal reinforcements that constrict and control the body.

Summer corset

1875-1880
Inv. 1920.1.968
Musée Galliera, Paris

51

The reinforcements are made from heavy-duty materials, such as whalebone, rush, crinoline, steel, and elasticized materials. Initially designed to be worn over clothing and later over lingerie, undergarments in this category are made from more elaborate fabrics than those used for lingerie, in order to be less conspicuous. Articles of corsetry are sometimes made to match an outfit or to go with specific pieces of lingerie such as the petticoat.

Bustles and corsets

1876-1877
Winter fashion, illustrated album
of the Grands Magasins du Louvre
Musée Galliera, Paris

Figurine déposée
Grands Magasins du Louvre.

HILD

TOURNURES ET CORSETS

Fig. 603 — TOURNURE en *nansouk*, forme très-élégante, pour robes demi-longues, ornée de trois volants et garnie au bas de deux riches broderies.............. **33 et 36** fr.

Fig. 604. — JUPON-TRAINE *indispensable pour robes longues*, double jupe à cinq volants; garni de deux broderies très-riches... **49** fr.
Le même, garni de dentelle........ **39** fr.
Longueur 1m *devant*, 1m50 *derrière*.

AVIS TRÈS IMPORTANT. — *Afin d'éviter des erreurs ou des retards, nous prions les Dames de vouloir bien mentionner sur leurs commandes* : Comptoir des Tournures et Corsets.

In this way corsetry is more closely associated with the world of fashion and its trends: it is not only more evident than lingerie (in particular during the Middle Ages, when corsetry was worn on top of the dress), corsetry is above all the basis for new silhouettes. As a result, corsetry was more roundly criticized than lingerie.

Morning
———
c. 1880
Cotton and lace, Inv. 1975.1.4
Musée Galliera, Paris

On one side were those who upheld corsetry as a symbol of a woman's morality, her physical posture evoking her upright behavior. On the other side were physicians, hygienists, and later feminists who accused designers and manufacturers of seeking to imprison the female body in a highly unnatural apparatus capable of causing physical damage.

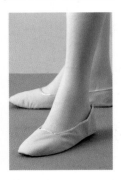

Combinations

English, c.1883-1895
white cotton with Bedfordshire Maltese
lace trimming corset, red satin
and steel wire bustle
Victoria and Albert Museum, London

That women agreed to wear the armatures, despite such criticisms, was more than a simple nod to fashion: for most it was a means of concealing their imperfections. The female body had long been considered lax and extra support was deemed necessary, as attested by Vogue in 1932: "Women's abdominal muscles are notoriously weak and even hard exercise does not keep your figure from spreading if you don't give it some support".

"A la Perséphone"

Anonymous, 1889
Poster, 55 x 43 cm
Bibliothèque Forney, Paris

A LA PERSÉPHONE

CORSETS DE PARIS

175332

Corsetry was every woman's ally, because it allowed her to hide the flaws she saw in her body and to emphasize her assets (at the price of a little suffering). That was the case for Caroline in Honoré de Balzac's *Petites misères de la vie conjugale* (Minor Tribulations of Married Life), who wore "her most deceptive corset." Lastly, corsetry (like lingerie) has a highly erotic quality, because it emphasizes the most emblematically feminine areas of a woman's body.

Four young women in dressing gown combination and pink nightdress

1890
Pages from *Art, Goût et Beauté*

Modéle n° 598. — Pyjama en crêpe-satin vert pour le pantalon, doublure du ton pour la casaque. Broderie de style oriental sur les manches. Volants en forme posés sous découpes donnant l'ampleur en jupe du pantalon.

Création DUPOUY-MAGNIN.

INTIMITÉ. Chemise de nuit en crêpe-satin. Travail de nids d'abeille et points de lingerie autour de l'encolure et sur les manches de forme pingouin.

Création ROUFF.

COQUETTERIE. — Combinaison dessous de robe en crêpe-satin et crêpe georgine Iris A.G.B. Le crêpe georgine Iris A.G.B. forme le soutien-gorge et le volant en forme en bas. Travail de jours en dentelures au bord du crêpe-satin.

Création ROUFF.

L'AURORE. — Combinaison-jupon en crêpe georgine Iris A.G.B. noir et dentelle ancienne ocrée. Travail de fils de fronces au milieu de la gorgerette. Haute ceinture. Panneaux plissés formant la jupe tout autour.

Création PREMET.

Our study would be incomplete without mentioning hosiery. This third category of women's underwear groups together the manufacture, industry, and business of knitwear, including stockings, socks, and certain articles of lingerie, such as underpants and undershirts. Hosiery is defined by its weave, which is based on a knit stitch using materials such as wool, cotton, silk, nylon, and contemporary microfibers.

Black corset embroidered with mauve

c.1890
Leloir Fund, Inv. 1986.59.16
Musée Galliera, Paris

The hosiery industry, which has undergone major technological changes related to advancements in looms and industrialization in the sector, completes the trilogy of women's underwear known as lingerie-corsetry-hosiery. During our era the distinction between the three categories has been largely non-existent, with frequent crossovers among the different groups (i.e. underwire bras, control-top panty hose, and "tummy control" briefs).

Thomson crinoline

Circles of metal and wicker with eyelets
Inv. 2003.74.X.
Musée Galliera, Paris

65

jetez votre cigare sur l
vous arrête comme ince

Indeed, contemporary underwear is the result of the evolution of these three categories. Their hygienic, shaping, and aesthetic functions come together in the underwear of the 21st century. Every period develops a design aesthetic that makes the preceding era appear outmoded. Women's undergarments play a fundamental role in the construction of a fashion silhouette. The reshaping takes place around the costume's main areas of support: shoulders, waist, bust, and hips.

"Corset counter"

1894
Advertisement
Musée Galliera, Paris

A LA

PLACE CLICHY

NOUVEAUTÉS

PARIS

— Vous jetez votre cigare sur le pavé gou-
dronné! Je vous arrête comme incendiaire.

A LA

PLACE CLICHY

NOUVEAUTÉS

PARIS

COMPTOIR DES CORSETS

CORSETS FAÇON

MANUFACTURE
MARQUE **L. G.** DÉPOSÉE
DE CORSETS

CORSETIÈRES

A LA RENOMMÉE

CORSET satin laine noir, éventaillé
couleur, très beau baleinage, forme
corsetière. **14.50**

CORSET en satin de laine noir, véritable baleine, garni haut et bas d'une
broderie sur même tissu. . **48.50**

CORSET en coutil de soie noir, article souple en véritable baleine. **27.—**

CORSET en satin laine noir, se fait
en véritable baleine, recommandé
pour sa solidité **15.50**

CORSET en coutil broché fond écru
souple, solide, élégant **8.90**

Grand choix de Corsets en tous genres et à tous prix.

The body was draped during Antiquity, which emphasized the figure. Such was the case in Egypt where undergarments were non-existent and the nude body moved freely underneath a tunic. Slaves, dancers, and musicians actually went completely nude to indicate their separate status from their masters, who wore a transparent tunic.

Underskirt

c.1897
Pink taffetas, satin ribbons
Belgerie donation, Inv.1979.77.1
Musée Galliera, Paris

Although the open attitude towards dress and the drape lasted into classical and Hellenistic Greece, femininity was suppressed with cloth bands that flattened chest and hips. Androgyny, which some attribute to the homosexual values of Greek civilization, governed the silhouette. The Hellenistic woman was completely covered up, her sexuality hidden under the folds of the chiffon.

"Les Bas de Soie"
(Silk Stockings)

Poster from Maison Doré Doré
Musées d'Art et d'Histoire, Troyes

MAISON DORÉ DORÉ
DORÉ et FILS Successeurs

Le Bas de Soie **DD** Bonneterie de Luxe

Roman civilization continued the war against curves. In a male-dominated society where women had no role, females were apparently prohibited from revealing their morphological traits. Some physicians even offered treatments to prevent an over-developed bust. Dioscorides advised applying a powder ground from Naxos stone to the breasts; Pliny suggested the mud used by knife-grinders; and Ovid recommended poultices of breadcrumbs soaked in milk.

"Corsets Baleinine Incassables"
(Unbreakable Whale Bone Corsets)

Alfred Choubrac, c.1900
Poster, 93 x 129 cm
Bibliothèque Forney, Paris

73

Although the effectiveness of these miracle cures is unknown, they do reflect contempt for the female figure and its softness, as well as a desire to repress the physical attributes of femininity. In the Middle Ages the silhouette was lean and the waist began to acquire definition. A cult of slenderness prevailed during the 14th and 15th centuries, achieved with close-fitting undergarments, and in particular the surcoat, which flattened the breasts, accentuated the curve of the lower back, and emphasized the stomach.

Black corset adourned with blue flowers

1900
Bourdy donation, Inv.1959.7.4
Musée Galliera, Paris

By the late Middle Ages, a period marked by serious epidemics of the plague, the round belly and its navel were appreciated as symbols of fertility and hope for a de-populated Europe. The English poet John Gower (1325-1403) evokes the preference for women with healthy bellies in the following lines: "Hee seeth hir shape forthwith all / Hir body round, hir middle small."

Corset concealer

———————

c.1900
Ivory lace
Musée Galliera, Paris

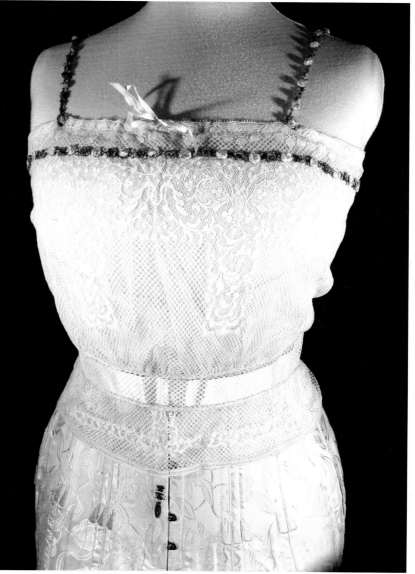

In contrast to the soft drape of Antiquity stiffness is now obtained from internal armatures that constricted and controlled the body.

16th century European costume is marked by a particular rigor of Spanish origin. The *vertugadin* or *vertugale* was an innovative undergarment meant to give fullness to the skirt.

Box of corset "à la Perséphone"

Musée Galliera, Paris

Adopted in England in the 1550s, where it was called the farthingale, it attained enormous girth by 1590; in Spain it lasted until 1625. The farthingale gave volume to the hips, exaggerated the stomach, and accentuated the curve of the back. Underneath it women wore bloomers (called "deceivers" when they were padded) that shaped thighs and buttocks and increased the skirt's volume.

"Un corset droit"
(Straight corset)

March 1903
Advertisement from the magazine *Les Modes*
Musée Galliera, Paris

UN CORSET DROIT, FORME NOUVELLE
DE LA M^{on} DE VERTUS SŒURS

The bust was funnel-shaped, stiffened by a bodice called a *basquine* that constricted the waist, hid the breasts, and flared out towards the shoulders.

In the 17th century women's breasts became round again, set off by whalebone bodies that rose high on the torso and reduced the size of the waist by tight lacing.

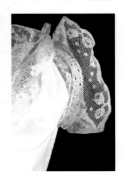

Corset concealer

c.1905
Cotton and lace with pink linen
Oberkampf donation, Inv. 1993.103.6
Musée Galliera, Paris

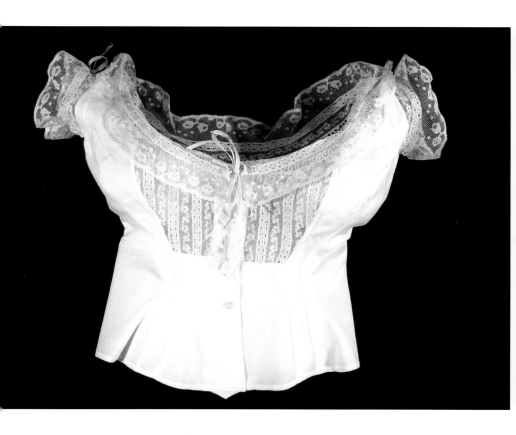

Around 1670, the bust was streamlined because the whalebone body extended much further below the waist in front and back. The whalebone body rose even higher in back during the 18th century, when little girls wore it at an early age. At the end of the 18th century, some women resorted to cheating on their proportions by hiding fake breasts inside the bodice.

Pair of embroidered socks

c.1905
Musée Galliera, Paris

85

The 17th century saw the farthingale replaced by the *robe volante*, or flying gown, enhanced with panniers. Panniers shaped skirts according to the rapidly changing fashion, appearing somewhat round in 1718, before becoming oval circa 1725, a shape they would retain until 1730. Panniers were later adapted to a multitude of forms, including the *panier à coude*, or pannier at elbow height, which extended far out from the sides.

Corset concealer and big underskirt

1906
Commercial catalogues from the
French department store Au Printemps
Musée Galliera, Paris

CACHE-CORSET en nansouck soyeux, jolie broderie et
dentelle, entre-deux et plis lingerie. . **16** fr. 90
GRAND JUPON en nansouck, deux volants jolie dentelle
et entre-deux, troutrou et ruban . **18** fr. 50

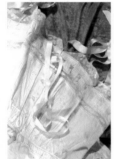

After 1740, the elbow pannier consisted of a pair of small panniers at each side, giving the skirt a flat appearance in front and behind, but making it very wide sideways. At the end of the 18th century, panniers were replaced by the bustle, a piece of corsetry worn in the rear to enhance or accentuate the figure's natural curves.

Slit underwear, corset concealer and combination

1906
Cotton cloth, lace and satin ribbon
Inv. 1972.12.1A/B/C
Musée Galliera, Paris

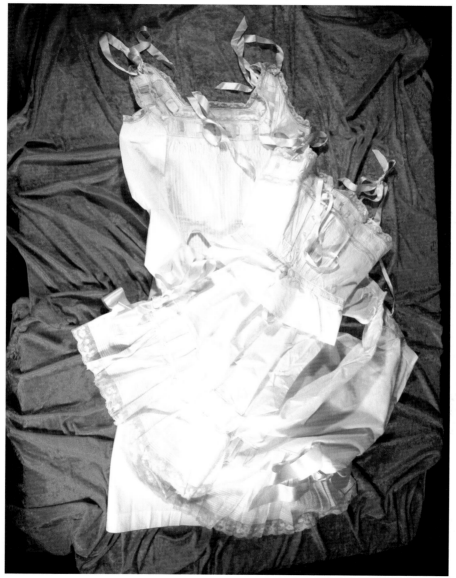

Beginning in 1770 the whalebone body was criticized by contemporaries such as Jean-Jacques Rousseau who advocated a return to simplicity and nature. Others launched veritable medical and educational crusades, like Bonnaud, author of 'The Degradation of the Human Race Through the Use of the Whalebone Corset' (1770).

"The Thylda corset, ideal hygienic corset of the Parisian woman"

December 1907
Les Modes
Musée Galliera, Paris

Photo Félix.

LE CORSET THYLDA
22, Place Vendôme. — PARIS

L'idéal corset hygiénique de la Parisienne.

Although nothing came of these condemnations (a small waist, large skirt, and generous bust remained in favor), fashion was set to return to a straight silhouette: the pannier had already given way to the bustle, which in turn gradually disappeared. From this trend a new slender style was born in France introduced by the elegant women known as *les Merveilleuses*, including Mme Récamier and Mme Tallien.

"The Thylda corset"

December 1907
Les Modes
Musée Galliera, Paris

The long, straight silhouette appeared in England with post-revolutionary immigrant Rose Bertin. The return of the Greek tunic marked fashion history's first revival. The silhouette is long, straight, and marked by a high waist.

Women's undergarments did not necessarily disappear, especially for those with less-than-perfect figures according to the canons of fashion.

Nightdress and costume underskirt

1908
Commercial catalogue from the
French department store Au Printemps
Musée Galliera, Paris

26499.

CHEMISE DE NUIT
linon soyeux, dentelle et entre-deux
très belle imitation, plis lingerie.   39 fr.

63101. JUPON DE COSTUME
en nansouk, volant à plis, garni entre-deux et dentelle imitation,
jour boutonnière et ruban. . . . .   59 fr.

In 1800 a corset was still needed to reduce curves, the most well-known corset makers being Lacrois and Furet, and the First Empire style with separated breasts introduced by Louis-Hippolyte Leroy made wearing one unavoidable. The corset *à la Ninon*, a waist-length, padded corset meant to create an ample figure, marked a return to a buxom, womanly ideal promoted by imperial politics.

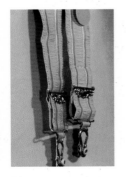

The "Furet" corset

1908
Galea donation, Inv.1962.108.225
Musée Galliera, Paris

The "divorce corset" (so named because it separated the breasts) introduced in 1816 continued the trend of distinctly separated breasts. The waist descended to its natural position. The Romantic woman's waist was accentuated by a laced corset. She wore a large skirt that flared into a bell-shape supported by a petticoat and puffed sleeves with armatures. Sloping shoulders were admired, emphasized by very low armholes.

"Corsets C.P. à la Sirène"
(C.P. corsets in the mermaid style)

Advertisement
Grands Magasins de la Samaritaine

Corsets
C. P. à la Sirène
PARIS

"Cavatine"

Corset très allongé du bas. Son système de pattes de jarretelles sur le devant permet toutes les positions du corps sans aucune gêne.

Ces articles sont en vente à Paris

Aux Grands Magasins de la SAMARITAINE

En Province et à l'Étranger, dans les Magasins de Nouveautés, Spécialité de Corsets, etc. Sinon s'adresser pour renseignements aux fabricants.

ÉTABLISSEMENTS
FARCY & OPPENHEIM
PARIS

The crinoline underskirt, originally a large bell shape, was round on the bottom and bulged slightly in the back. After 1860 it grew much longer in the back giving the appearance of a large flare. But by 1868 the crinoline had fallen victim to its own extremes and was reduced to a simple cone shape that would evolve into the bustle that only protruded in the rear.

Cover for the commercial catalogue
Comptoir des Corsets

A. Rapeno, Winter 1913-1914
Grands Magasins du Louvre
Musée Galliera, Paris

LOUVRE

PARIS   COMPTOIR DES Corsets

Tout PLUS ÉLÉGANT et MEILLEUR MARCHÉ que partout ailleurs

101

Around 1865-1870 the silhouette became less voluminous. The bustle or "Parisian bum" marked the curve of the lower back and enabled the skirt's flounces to be kept in back. The front was very flat, due to a high corset containing the bust. These waist-reducing corsets gave the female body an hourglass shape.

"La Belle Matineuse"
(The Beautiful Morning)

1914
Modes et manières d'Aujourd'hui
Musée Galliera, Paris

G. BARBIER 1914

La Belle Matineuse

Je t'ai connue à ton matin, ô belle Matineuse! Souviens-toi.....

This was the era of the great debates over the corset's beneficial or detrimental effects, part of a larger debate on the unfair status of women. Some women, such as the American journalist Amalia Bloomer, attempted to design a "rational dress" made up of a short, tunic-style dress worn over bloomers, but the bloomers met with ridicule and women's clothing continued to emphasize curves.

"Corsets pour enfants et fillettes"
(Corsets for children and young girls)

Winter 1913-1914
Grands Magasins du Louvre
Musée Galliera, Paris

CORSETS pour ENFANTS et FILLETTES

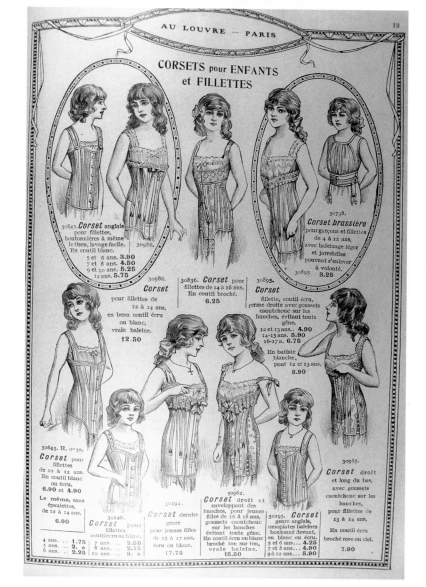

30645. *Corset anglais*
pour fillettes,
boutonnières à même
le tissu, lavage facile.
En coutil blanc.

5 et 6 ans. **3.90**
7 et 8 ans. **4.50**
9 et 10 ans. **5.25**
12 ans. **5.75**

30738.
Corset brassière
pour garçons et fillettes
de 4 à 12 ans,
avec baleinage léger
et jarretelles
pouvant s'enlever
à volonté.
30895 **3.25**

30986.
Corset
pour fillettes de
12 à 14 ans,
en beau coutil écru
ou blanc,
vraie baleine.
12.50

30836. *Corset* pour
fillettes de 14 à 16 ans.
En coutil broché.
6.25

30895.
Corset
fillette, coutil écru,
forme droite avec goussets
caoutchouc sur les
hanches, évitant toute
gêne.

12 et 13 ans. **4.90**
14-15 ans. **5.90**
16-17 a. **6.75**

En batiste
blanche,
pour 12 et 13 ans.
8.90

30643. H. 0m30.
Corset pour
fillettes
de 10 à 12 ans.
En coutil blanc
ou écru.
6.90 et **4.90**
Le même, sans
épaulettes,
de 12 à 14 ans.
6.90

30128.
Corset pour
fillettes
coutil écru ou blanc.

4 ans... **1.75**
5 ans... **2.»**
6 ans... **2.25**
7 ans... **2.50**
8 ans... **2.75**
10 ans... **3.»**

30194.
Corset dernier
genre
pour jeunes filles
de 15 à 17 ans,
écru ou blanc.
17.75

30962.
Corset droit et
enveloppant des
hanches, pour jeunes
filles de 16 à 18 ans,
goussets caoutchouc
sur les hanches
évitant toute gêne.
En coutil écru ou blanc
broché ton sur ton,
vraie baleine.
15.50

30195. *Corset*
genre anglais,
omoplates baleines
boutonné devant,
en blanc ou écru.
5 et 6 ans... **4.25**
7 et 8 ans... **4.90**
9 à 12 ans... **5.90**

30985.
Corset droit
et long du bas,
avec goussets
caoutchouc sur les
hanches,
pour fillettes de
13 à 14 ans.
En coutil écru
broché rose ou ciel.
7.90

105

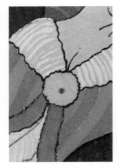

In the 1880s the front of the silhouette was increasingly emphasized, thanks to corsets with long metallic stiffeners that diminished the stomach and constricted bust and hips. From 1880-1905 a woman's body was physically distorted into an "S" shape: her bust was pushed forward, while her hips and buttocks were propelled backwards.

"Les coussins"
(The Cushions)

Musée Galliera, Paris

Voici l'heure entre toutes si délicate,
Si délicate et précieuse, où l'on goûte
Les minutes qui s'égrennent goutte à goutte
Comme un collier de turquoises et d'agates.

The bust was low, ample, and undivided, which gave a look of grandiloquence sometimes enhanced with artificial breasts made of chamois leather, quilted satin, or rubber. The bustle raised the buttocks and defined the small of the back. This new serpentine silhouette corresponds to the arabesques of Art Nouveau.

Cover for the commercial catalogue
A la chaussée d'Antin

———————

Charles Hérouard, 1917
27 x 22 cm
Bibliothèque Forney, Paris

1917

Imprimerie d'Art & Bulletin   Chland Marenne & C⁰ . Paris   HERQUARD

In response to the sinuous silhouette, Doctor Franz Glénard and Mme Gaches-Sarraute, a corset-maker with a medical background, introduced new corsets to give the thorax more freedom. These models supported the abdomen without constricting it, while liberating the chest and diaphragm. Anglo-Saxon anti-corset leagues sprang up in the same spirit with the goal of rationalizing the costume.

Excerpt from the catalogue of Yva Richard

c.1920
Stencil watercolour, 22 x 16 cm
Private collection, Paris

"JOLI RIEN"

YVA RICHARD
8, RUE DU MARCHÉ SAINT-HONORÉ
7, RUE SAINT-HYACINTHE, PARIS, 1ᵉ A¹
R.C. SEINE 98.703. TÉLÉPH CENTRAL 00·69

Authorities in several countries spoke out against corset wearing. This war against the corset (the control of women's bodies having long been associated with moral preservation) finds an echo in the women's suffrage movement in England that sought equal rights for women. By 1907 the "S" silhouette was losing ground and gave way to a more refined look that harked back to Empire styles.

Ladies underwear

Yva Richard, c.1920
Silver print, 18 x 13 cm
Private collection, Paris

The new silhouette had a high waist, diminished bust, and narrow hips, giving the woman a tube-like appearance. Although this new style marked the end of the tightly laced waist, it required straight hips and flat buttocks, hence a corset that was flat and rigid in the front worn low on the hips. Softness was restored to the bust, thanks to the invention of the brassière.

Postcard with unwritten back

Yva Richard, c.1920
14 x 9 cm
Private collection, Paris

Slenderness remained essential. According to 1922 Vogue, "the pursuit of slimness is one of the chief labors of the modern woman."

The idea of physical ease was also promoted by theatrical productions in which performers moved their bodies freely on stage. Performances like those by *Les Ballets Russes*, which were produced at the Théâtre du Châtelet in 1909, and by dancer Isadora Duncan met with great success.

"Lingerie", Martial and Armand creations

Art, Goût Beauté, May 1925
Musée Galliera, Paris

LINGERIE

✦ ✦ ✦

Créations Martial et Armand

Parure en Supercrêpe A. G. B.

Aware of these changes, couturiers Paul Poiret, Madeleine Vionnet, and Nicole Groult helped abolish the sinuous silhouette. Their innovations coincided with the new Latin and American dance crazes (tango and Charleston), which relied on an unrestricted body. The emergence of a working middle class in need of more functional apparel gave additional impetus to streamlined styles.

Bouclette and Her Corset

Yva Richard, c.1925
Silver print, 17.6 x 13 cm
Alexandre Dupouy collection, Paris

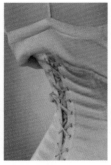

With the First World War (1914-18) the silhouette was further simplified and volume was abandoned. Nevertheless, only the thinnest women were among those brave enough to abandon their corset. For other women, an invisible, scaled-down corset became available. In the 1920s women wore a style of knee-length dress that made breasts and waist disappear.

Wyndham no.176

c. 1925
Postcard with printed back, 14 x 9 cm
Private collection, Paris

121

An ample bust was no longer an issue, as women were wearing brassières, including smooth, long-line models that flattened the breasts Roman style. Curves made a come back at the end of the decade and the bust, now defined and accentuated, required armatures for support.

Bra

—

Presented at the Exposition des Arts décoratifs, 1925
Embroidered feather, lace, cotton and satin
Andreeff donation, Inv. 1947.49.
Musée Galliera, Paris

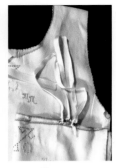

The Kestos company introduced a new concept bra that offered control without restricting the breasts: if women were going to continue wearing corsetry, it would have to have greater ease. Thanks to a better understanding of human anatomy, corsetry began to follow the body's natural contours.

Ensemble
_____

c.1925
Yellow cotton with mauve and green embroidery
Marot donation, Inv. 1987.33.3A/B/C
Musée Galliera, Paris

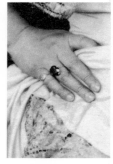

In Australia, the Berlei company commissioned two Sydney University professors to undertake the first anthropometric study of female body types. They defined five, thereby demonstrating the variety of morphologies. Warner innovated in the measurement of cups with A, B, C, and D sizes.

Postcard with unwritten back

Yva Richard, c.1925
14 x 9 cm
Private collection, Paris

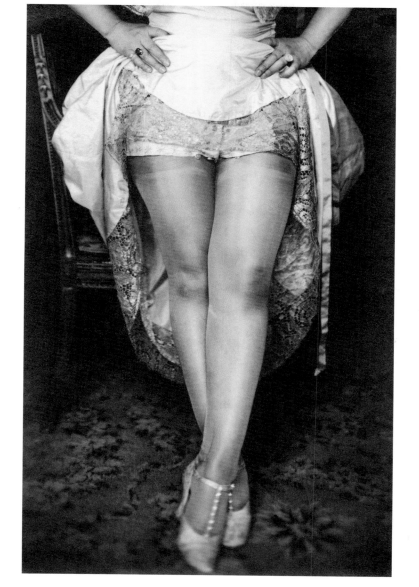

127

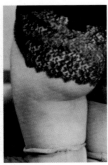

The "Flapper" look went out of fashion in the early 1930s and manufacturers tried to address the diversity of female shapes by offering a wide variety of sizes. The high bust of the post-Second World War era made its first appearance in 1930, supported by brassières and corsets with round and pointed cups.

Cover for the fifth edition
of the French magazine *Frivolités*

Arès Editions, c.1925
Silver prints
Private collection, Paris

FRiVOLiTÉS

No 5

In 1935 brassières were updated with padded cups to flatter small breasts and three years later underwire bras were introduced that gave a protruding bustline. There was also a return to a small waist achieved with girdles.

The 1940s woman was thin, but had curvaceous hips and breasts that were pointy and shapely.

"Au corset de Vénus"
(The corset of Venus)

c.1925
Advertisement slot, front side
Musée Galliera, Paris

She was aided by a new brassière with topstitched cups and sometimes reinforced tips. During the 1940s, the bust was elevated for the torso-hugging sweater look. In order to achieve a thin waist and a flat stomach, Marcel Rochas introduced the guêpière. The fashion was for the "New Look," a silhouette created by Christian Dior in 1947 based on a voluminous skirt, wasp waist, and large bust.

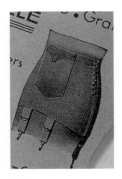

"Au corset de Vénus"
(The corset of Venus)

c.1925
Advertisment slot, back side
Musée Galliera, Paris

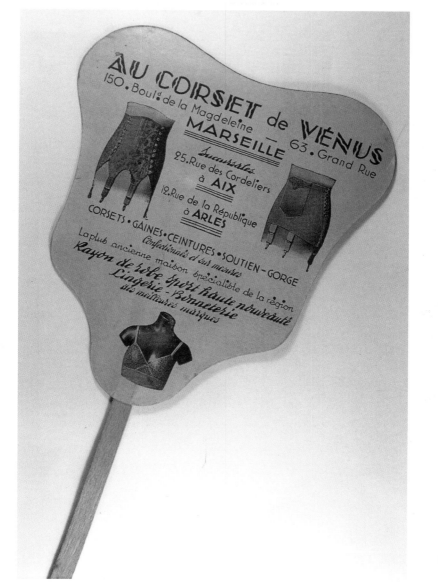

133

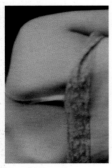

In the early 1950s, the silhouette appeared longer with high breasts, a small bust, and an accent on the hollow of the stomach. Corsetry and padding were required. Newspapers promoted the benefits of proper diet and exercise in addition to a good piece of corsetry. The 1950s also witnessed a fashion for the overdeveloped bust, either cylindrical (the bombshell) or spherical in shape, obtained with topstitched brassières.

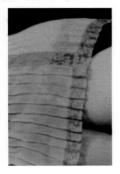

Ladies underwear

Anonymous, c.1925
Silver print, 6 x 15.5 cm
Private collection, Paris

This was the image promoted by actresses such as Anita Ekberg, Gina Lollobrigida, Sophia Loren, Jane Mansfield, Marilyn Monroe, and Jane Russell. The manufacturers Marcel Carlier, Carles Krafft, Jessos, Scandale, and Star produced corsetry with reinforcements for the full-figured "goddess."

The Corset

Albert Wyndham, c.1925
Silver print, 23.6 x 17.5 cm
Private collection, Paris

137

In the 1960s the female silhouette was liberated along with social mores. The look was adolescent breasts, slim hips, and extreme thinness. André Courrèges was the first to make a fashion statement out of the youth culture when his 1965 collection presented androgynous figures and the image of a modern woman comfortable with her own body.

"Les sous vêtements. Les chemises sport, véritable tissus"
(Underwear. Sport shirts, real fabric)

Anonymous, c.1930
Advertiment board, 22 x 18 cm
Bibliothèque Forney, Paris

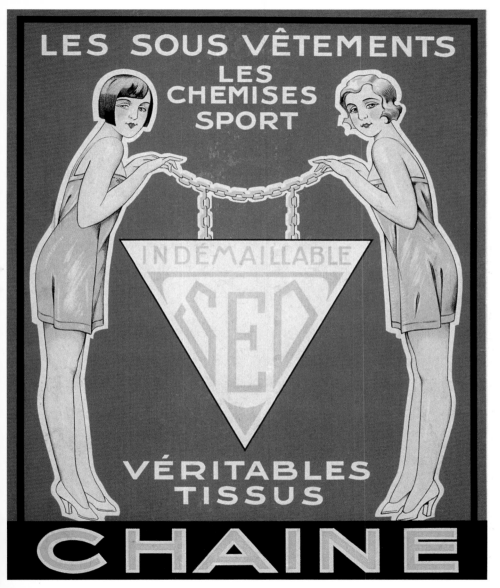

Women's undergarments, in particular underpants, followed the body's own contours. By the end of the decade, after the uprisings of '68 and the bra-burning Women's Liberation movement, women's breasts were emancipated under tight-fighting pullovers and Indian tunics. Fashion had gone from a complex array of undergarments to almost nothing.

Untitled

Atelier Edith Barakovich, c.1930
Silver print, 16 x 21.5 cm
Private collection, Paris

Leggy women with small breasts, such as Jane Birkin and the model Twiggy, were popular. After the hippie trend, fashion advocated a return to sophistication, in other words, a return to femininity. Toning and stretching exercises were popular as women demonstrated an obsessive desire to be thin and to sculpt the body firm.

Illustration from the first edition
of the magazine *Roussel*

1933
Private collection, Paris

The 1980s woman exchanged control panties, girdles, and corsets for weight lifting and diet pills. The armature became internal, with the woman acting as her own corset. At the same time, breasts had to be generous and firm. The fashion image of thin waist-muscular buttocks-protruding breasts defined feminine beauty and required padded, underwire bras for those who were not "naturally" endowed.

Illustration from the first edition
of the magazine *Roussel*

1933
Private collection, Paris

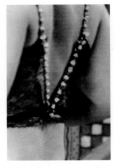

An ambiguous silhouette arose in late 20th century that was extremely tall and thin with narrow hips – and big breasts. In short, a woman that was simultaneously adolescent and sexual. These demands were obviously hard to reconcile, requiring draconian diets, padded bras, and even plastic surgery.

Untitled

———

Yva Richard, c. 1935
Silver print, 17.5 x 12.8 cm
Private collection, Paris

Glossary
Baby doll

A very short nightgown introduced in the 1950's made of sheer fabrics, usually nylon, but sometimes silk or cotton.

Batiste

Batiste (also called handkerchief linen). A fine fabric of sheer bleached linen.

"Arwa"

Anonymous, c.1935
Poster, 89 x 63 cm
Bibliothèque Forney, Paris

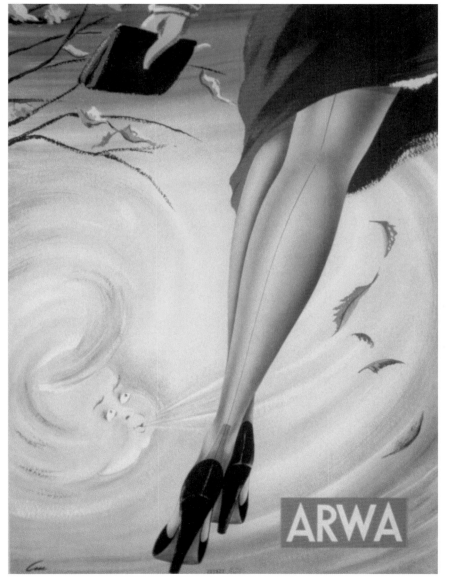

Bikini

A style of underpants.

Bloomers

Long pants that fall to the ankle, or stop at the calf or thigh. Bloomers come in linen or cotton; later more refined versions are made of silk and decorated with embroidery, lace, and ribbon.

Diana slip

c.1935
Silver print, 16 x 11 cm
Private collection, Paris

6

Body Stocking

Borrowed from the leotards worn by dancers and female athletes, the body stocking is a close-fitting article of clothing that encases the torso. It is designed to button at the crotch for ease of use. A body stocking may have long or short sleeves and is made of cotton, lace, or synthetic fabrics. It can be worn as an under or outer garment.

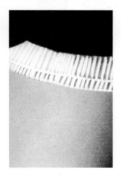

Diana slip

c.1935
Silver print, 16 x 11 cm
Private collection, Paris

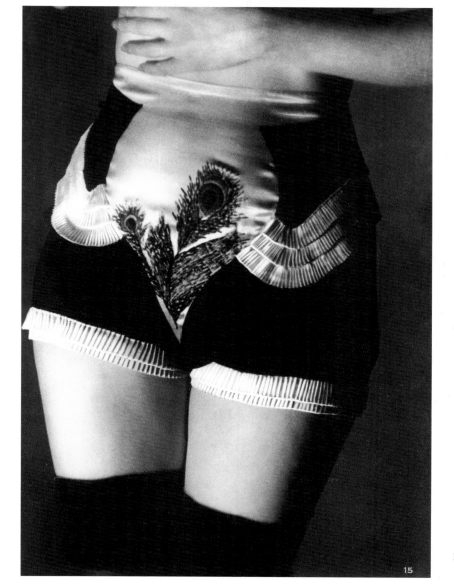

15

Brassiere

Underwear designed to support and enhance the breasts with or without underwiring. Simultaneously items of lingerie and corsetry, brassières were not commonly worn before the 1920s. Several individuals introduced models of brassières at the Paris World's Fair in 1900: Samaritaine's *Idéal* and *Mamellia*, Madame Cadolle's *Corselet-gorge* (brassière), and Madame Gaches-Sarraute's *Sans-gêne* (comfort), *Expansible* (stretch), and other models.

"Pommes d'amour"
(Love apples)

E. Klemm, c.1938
Catalogue *Diana Slip*, plate no.20
Private collection, Paris

155

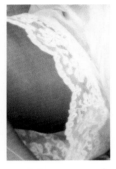

Hermine Cadolle had actually shown her first brassière in 1889, but there were problems with the support that had to be worked out. Maison Cadolle's first brassière was *Bien-Etre* (well-being), which was still attached to a corset in the back. In 1913, Caresse Crosby (a pseudonyme for Mary Phelps Jacob) produced a new type of short brassière in the United States that separated the breasts.

Ladies underwear

Yva Richard, c.1938
Silver print, 16 x 11 cm
Private collection, Paris

She sold her patent in 1914 to Warner Bros. Rosalind Kind (head of the Kestos label) perfected a brassière consisting of two triangles that crossed in front and back during the same era. The term brassière appeared in the Oxford Dictionary in 1912 but the shortened form "bra" only appeared after 1937. In France, the word *soutien-gorge* (brassière) entered the dictionary in 1923.

"The Seducer"

E. Klemm, c.1938
Catalogue *Diana Slip*, plate no.8
Private collection, Paris

159

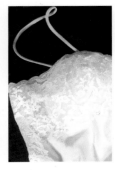

Bustle

Padding worn underneath the dress in the back at the level of the lower back and consisting of a half-cage whalebone armature that supported a bum roll (the bulky drapery formed by the rear part of the skirt). The bustle succeeded the crinoline around 1867, then disappeared around 1899. In France it was commonly called a *faux cul* (false rump).

Slip dress

1955-1960
Musée Galliera, Paris

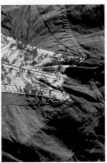

Corset

Although more flexible than the whalebone body, the corset was made from heavy fabric and was stiffened and laced. It gave shape to the silhouette and the dress by constricting the waist and the stomach and by molding the breasts. It could be highly ornate.

Corset cover

A piece of lingerie worn over the corset to conceal it.

Black basque

1955-60
Saglio donation, Inv. 1993.265.2
Musée Galliera, Paris

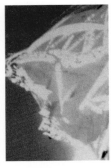

Cretonne

The name derives from Creton, a village in the Eure region of France. Cretonne fabric is a hard-wearing linen or cotton.

"Ciel de France"
(The sky of France)

Pierre Brenot, 1959
Advertisement for lingerie and stockings
43 x 32 cm
Bibliothèque Forney, Paris

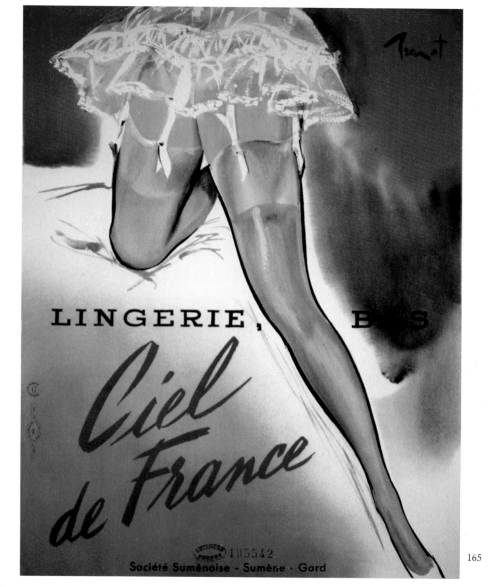

LINGERIE, BAS

Ciel de France

Brenot

105542

Société Suménoise - Sumène - Gard

165

Crinoline

The term originally referred to the material used for petticoats worn to support the widening skirts of the 1840's. This rigid fabric invented in 1840 by Oudinot to stiffen stocks worn by the military owes its name to the French word for horsehair (*crin*), from which it is woven. The crinoline or hoop skirt is an underskirt with a cage-like armature made from whalebone or spring steel hoops that women wore to make their dresses billow out.

Négligé

———

Dior, c.1960
White lace and rose satin bows
Martini donation, Inv. 2003.77.1A/B
Musée Galliera, Paris

Dimity

A common fabric characterized by a linen or hemp warp and a cotton weft in use since the 13th century.

Dressing gown (also called a robe)

In the 17th century, dressing gown meant something other than court dress that one could wear at home excluding receiving guests. It was not yet a lounging robe, except for men. In the 19th century the woman's dressing gown became the lounging robe known as a negligee. It is generally worn upon rising and retiring to hide the nightgown or pajamas and may be made from all sorts of textiles.

Ensemble of red tartan

Princesse Tam-Tam, before 1995

169

Embroidery

Decorative needlework using thread that more or less covers the material. Embroidered motifs may be flat or raised, openwork, geometric, floral, or animal. Embroidery thread may be linen, cotton, ramie, rayon, silk, wool, or synthetic and metallic filaments sheathed in polyester. Some embroidered designs include pearls and sequins, lace, soutaches, ribbons, and fabric appliqué. Embroidery can be done by hand or by machine.

Princesse Tam-Tam advertisement

1996

Vous êtes en territoire Princesse Tam-Tam,
attention nombre
d'ethnologues n'en sont jamais revenus.

Farthingale (vertugadin or vertugade)

A stiff, bell-shaped petticoat stretched over large iron wires or wooden sticks. Spanish in origin, the farthingale was designed to make the skirt flare. French fashion transformed it into a round bolster positioned at the waist that distributed the fullness of the dress around the body. At the end of the 16th century, the farthingale took yet another form when it became a wheel upon which the skirt extended.

Princesse Tam-Tam advertisement

Fall/Winter 1997

Complètement Tam-Tam cette Princesse.

Princesse
TAM·TAM
PARIS

Filling (also called weft, woof, or pick)

Threads passed perpendicular to the warp thread during the weaving process.

Flannel

A soft and fleecy, loosely woven fabric made from worsted or carded wool.

Ensemble of bra and pants

Princesse Tam-Tam, Fall/Winter 1998-1999
"Cocooning" collection

French panty and pettipants

In France the term panty refers to a control panty with legs made from an elasticized stretch material. Use of the French panty spread during the 1960's. The form was adapted to lingerie fashions and called pettipants, in which case the legs are loose-fitting and decorated with lace at the extremities.

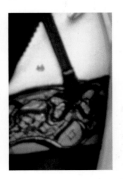

Ensemble

———————

Chantal Thomass
Fall/Winter 2001-2002

Fustian

A twill with a cotton weft and a different textile fiber (hemp, linen, or wool) for the warp.

Garter belt

Small accessory item resembling a belt made of rubberized ribbons, belts, or fabric strips (elasticized or not) with four garters for attaching stockings. The garter belt appeared around 1910.

Ensemble in white lace

Chantal Thomass
Fall/Winter 2001-2002

179

Garters (bands)

Belts or fabric bands (elasticized or not) worn around the legs above or below the knee to hold stockings up. Garters bands may be adorned with trimmings such as gold or silver fasteners, gems, and embroidery. Garter straps replaced garter bands in the 1900s.

Nuisette

Chantal Thomass
Fall/Winter 2001-2002

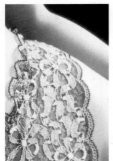

Garters (straps)

Elasticized strips or rubberized ribbon incorpo-
rated into a full girdle or garter belt (and into
underpants in some contemporary designs) and
with a small clip at the end for holding up stockings stretched over the legs. In addition, the
garter functions as a tensor near the top,
because it creates a straight line up to the corset.

Ensemble

———

Chantal Thomass
Fall/Winter 2001-2002

183

Girdle

Undergarment of elasticized material that fits tightly around the waist, hips, and sometimes the upper thighs. The girdle replaced the corset beginning in the 1930's.

Ensemble

––––––––––

Chantal Thomass
Fall/Winter 2001-2002

Guêpière (also called French cinch, waist-cincher, and waspie)

A type of girdle made from elasticized materials to make the waist look slimmer invented in 1946 by Marcel Rochas.

Jersey

Jersey is knit with a single weft yarn, which produces uniform stitches on one face. Jersey may be knit from cotton or silk.

Ensemble

Chantal Thomass
Fall/Winter 2001-2002

Lace

A delicate openwork fabric in which warp and weft threads are indistinguishable. Lace fabric consists of a net ground (mesh) and motifs obtained by interlacing, twisting, looping, or braiding threads. Lace can be made from linen, cotton, ramie, silk, rayon, wool, or metallic and synthetic threads. There are different varieties of lace. Bobbin lace is made by taking threads attached to small bobbins and interlacing them at specific points indicated by pins attached to a backing; Chantilly and Valenciennes are important bobbin lace-making centres.

Ensemble

Chantal Thomass
Fall/Winter 2001-2002

Needle lace, such as the Alençon and Venetian varieties, consists of a network of loops covered in stitches made with the needle; the technique actually comes from the refinement of openwork embroidery. Almost all contemporary lace is machine made. Machine made lace usually imitates traditional motifs and is manufactured in former handmade lace centres, such as Valenciennes and Chantilly.

Corset

———

Axfords

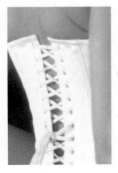

Lawn

A diaphanous plain weave fabric woven from linen or cotton that is finer than batiste.

Lycra and Lastex

A registered trademark introduced in 1959 after the material was invented in the laboratories of Dupont USA. Lycra is a synthetic fabric with a highly elastic network having the same properties as Lastex. Lastex, an elastic yarn invented in 1942 (the trademark derives from the words latex and elastic), is spun from rubber covered with natural or artificial textile fibers, hence its elasticity.

Wedding corset

Axfords

Mastodeton

An assemblage of ribbons tied around the breasts that served as a brassière in ancient Greece. The term comes from the Greek word for breast (*mastos*).

Moiré

A finishing technique used on ribbed fabrics after weaving. The fabric width is folded over (selvage on selvage) and subjected to heavy pressure, which crushes the ribs against each other. The result is a flattening of network and nap into a shiny surface. Moiré produces a shimmering pattern with more or less random outlines.

Corsets

———

Axfords

Muslin

A fine, lightweight, lustrous cloth that is usually finished. Muslin can be made from cotton, as well as wool and silk.

Negligee

An article of clothing made from fine fabric and worn in the home as loungewear and sometimes for receiving a few close friends that is especially associated with the 19th century.

Corsets

Axfords

Nightgown

Identical to the undershirt, but meant for sleeping. It may have long or short sleeves, or even straps. It is made of the same materials as the undershirt.

Nylon

A registered American trade name created in 1935 from the designation "no run" (meaning will not unravel). Nylon is a synthetic fiber (polyamide) obtained from the chemical interactions of tar by-products. It makes a hard-wearing, elastic, easy care material.

Combination from the line "Jet Set"

Barbara Creation
Fall/Winter 2003-2004

Nylon was developed by Du Pont de Nemours, Inc. Research began in 1927 and was successfully concluded by Dr. Wallace H. Carothers and his team in 1937. The first nylon stockings were displayed at the New York World's Fair that same year and went on sale in 1939. Nylon arrived in Great Britain in 1940 and was distributed by British Nylon Spinners Ltd. From 1947 nylon was being used extensively, enabling effects previously only obtained with costly materials.

Bustier bra with removable straps "Mystérieux"

Ravage
Fall/Winter 2003-2004

Pajamas

The term pajamas comes from the Hindustani word *pay-jamah* meaning leg garment. Pajamas are loose, lightweight garments consisting of a top (jacket) and bottom (pants) intended to be worn as nightclothes. Pajamas have been worn by both sexes since the 1920s, when women adopted a version that was more feminine in cut, patterns, and colors. The term can also refer to a beach outfit.

Ensemble "Attitude"

Chantelle, Fall/Winter 2003
Shell under wire bra and hidden under wire panties

Pannier

(also called hoops or hoop petticoat)

The body of a skirt stiffened with a rigid armature of rush or whalebone that was used to give
fullness to a dress or a skirt. Hoops come in
various shapes (round, oval, etc.).

Ensemble "Tamarine"

Chantelle, Fall/Winter 2003
Underwire bra and boxer short

Petticoat

An article of lingerie. In the beginning a petticoat was a short skirt worn under other skirts. At the end of the 18th century, petticoat referred to the skirt over which the dress opened up. By the late 19th century, the term petticoat was used to mean an article of intimate apparel. Several petticoats could be worn one on top of another. At first they were made of linen, then cotton, silk, or tulle. The petticoat was worn under panniers and crinolines. In 20th century, the petticoat was used to give volume to a skirt.

Ensemble "Yasmine"

Chantelle, Fall/Winter 2003
Basket bra and panties

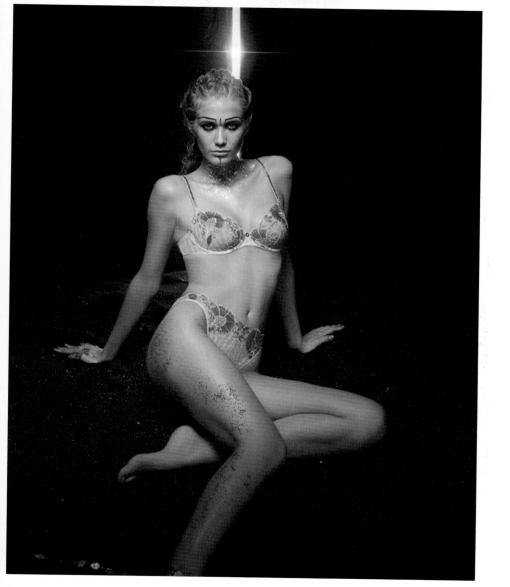

Plain weave (also called taffeta weave)

A weave with a simple structure in which filling threads alternate moving over and under warp threads. At each pick, one warp thread is successively passed under or floated over. As a result, both faces of a plain weave fabric are identical. Any textile can be woven in a plain weave: linen, cotton, petticoat linen, silk, man-made, and synthetic fibers.

Poplin

A taffeta weave fabric with silk warp and wool weft. An analogous cotton fabric with a taffeta weave has also come to be called poplin.

Ensemble "Volupté"

Chantelle, Fall/Winter 2003
Underwire bra and panties

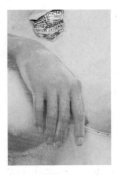

Rayon

Rayon got its name from the English and French words for ray because of its sheen. Rayon is produced from man-made (cellulose) fibers to make long filament, which is a distinctly different yarn from the short staple called spun rayon.

Ensemble "Maestria"

Chantelle, Fall/Winter 2003
Corset and panties

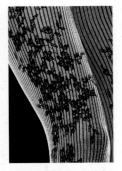

Rayon is sometimes called "artificial silk." Sir Joseph Swan was trying to invent a carbon filament for light bulbs in 1833 when his wife salvaged the fiber he created and began making crocheted articles. Three chemists named Crown, Bevan, and Beadle later formulated viscose rayon and registered their first patent in 1892.

Striped tights

Chantal Thomass
Fall/Winter 2003

Rayon production began in Great Britain in 1905 and in the United States in 1911, thanks to the support of Samuel Courtauld. Dr. Dreyfus perfected a method for producing acetate rayon, which British Celanese began developing in 1911. However, rayon was not actually utilized until after the 1920's.

Striped tights

Chantal Thomass
Fall/Winter 2003

Ribbon

A narrow band of fabric used for ornament or as a tie. Ribbons may be woven from cotton or silk in plain, silk, or pile weave.

Satin

In a satin weave, filling threads float over multiple warp threads with a step number of several threads from one pick to another. The staggered arrangement of the intersections inhibits the formation of ribs and gives this weave its smooth and lustrous appearance.

"Crystal" model

Yaël Landman
Fall/Winter 2003

The effect obtained is therefore different on each face, because one series of threads is more visible than the other. For example, on the dominant weft face of a satin weave with a harness number of 5, 4 warp threads are floated over and 1 passed under; on the warp face, 4 weft threads are passed under and 1 is floated over; the step number may be 2 or 3 threads from one pick to another. There are also satin weaves with harness numbers of 7 and 8 produced according to the same principle. This weave is suitable for silk, rayon fabrics (especially for lingerie), cotton, or wool.

"Fever" model

Yaël Landman
Fall/Winter 2003

Slip

An article of lingerie consisting of a top that generally has straps and a bottom in the form of a skirt. Slips come in variable lengths in cotton, silk, rayon, or nylon.

Socks

Articles of clothing made from knitted fabric that cover feet and lower legs and which can be of variable length. Socks come in wool, cotton, nylon, or fabric blends with spandex.

"Funky" model

Yaël Landman
Fall/Winter 2003

Stay

A small flexible strip used to support articles of corsetry. Stays may be bone, horn, metal (primarily steel), or plastic. The French term for stay is *baleine* (whalebone), because cetacean whalebones were long used for this purpose.

"Initials" model

Yaël Landman
Fall/Winter 2003

Stockings

The French term for stockings (*bas*) is short for *bas de chausse,* a close-fitting article of men's clothing that covered the leg from foot to knee. The term still means supple pieces of hosiery that cover the leg and the foot. More specifically, women's stockings cover the foot and the leg up to the thigh. They may be in wool, cotton, silk, rayon, or artificial silk.

"Michael" model

Yaël Landman
Fall/Winter 2003

String bikini

Minuscule panties similar to a G-string, the string bikini consists of a piece of fabric (or other material) over the front and a system of thin cords that leaves buttocks visible from behind.

Strophium

An ancient ancestor of the brassière, the Roman strophium was a scarf rolled into a sash and wrapped around the bust to support the breasts.

"Santino" model

Yaël Landman
Fall/Winter 2003

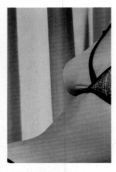

Taffeta

A silk fabric with a plain weave and with which scintillating effects can be obtained by using different coloured threads for warp and filling, whence the phrase shimmering taffeta.

"Vito" model

Yaël Landman
Fall/Winter 2003

Tights

Very tight-fitting (hence its name) article of clothing made from knitted fabric that covers the body from feet to waist where it is held up by elastic. Tights can be made from wool, cotton, silk, rayon, artificial silk, or nylon.

"Up" stockings

Chantal Thomass
Fall/Winter 2003

Twill

In a twill weave the filling threads float over several warp threads with a step number of one thread from one pick to another. The intersections of a twill weave therefore form diagonal lines slanting left (S motif) or right (Z motif).

Plumetis tights

Chantal Thomass
Fall/Winter 2003

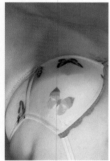

The two faces of a twill fabric differ, because one series of threads is more visible than the other. On the dominant warp face, warp threads float over weft threads; on the weft face, weft threads float over the warp threads.

Bra and pantie

Wonderbra

A twill with a harness number of 3 refers to a twill weave in which three threads are floated over and one thread passed under during weaving, but there are also twills with harness numbers of 4 and 5. Any textile can be made with a twill weave and varying degrees of brightness and sheen can be obtained thanks to the floats. Twill is the weave used to make jeans.

Bra and panties ensemble

La Perla, Fall/Winter 2003

Underpants (also called pants, panties, briefs, drawers, and unmentionables)
Underwear that covers the lower trunk with two opening for the legs. Underpants are made from a multitude of textiles, including cotton, silk, and nylon, and may be decorated with embroidery, lace, ribbons, or other trim.

Band bra

La Perla

239

Undershirt

An article of lingerie that covers the upper body and varies in length according to the epoch. The undershirt is worn under corsetry items like a second skin. Originally made from linen cloth, it later became more refined in cotton, silk, or nylon decorated with lace, ribbons, or embroidery.

Voile

A fine sheer fabric with a plain weave woven from cotton, wool, or silk.

Body

———

La Perla
Fall/Winter 2003

Warp

Threads stretched lengthwise parallel to the loom and between which filling threads (weft) are interlaced during the weaving process.

Weave

The method of interlacing warp and weft threads that technically determines the character of a woven fabric.

"Paradise Lace" corsage

Worlford
Summer 2004

Whalebone body
(corps à baleine or corps)

An article of corsetry worn from the 16th to 18th centuries that bound the bust by incorporating whalebone stays into a tightly-laced bodice. It was replaced by the corset. The whalebone body was made of heavy-duty fabrics often decorated with more costly textiles on the exterior.

"Bohème"

———

Wolford
Spring/Summer 2004

Zona

A Greek foundation garment dating to the 9th century BC, the zona was a large belt designed for young girls to be worn over the hips until marriage.

Stocking belt

Wolford
Spring/Summer 2004

Index